Dancing with the Sunbeams

Nistha Nautiyal

BookLeaf Publishing

India | USA | UK

Presentation by *BookLeaf Publishing*

Web: www.bookleafpub.com

E-mail: info@bookleafpub.com

ISBN: 9789363306622

First edition 2024

ACKNOWLEDGEMENT

I am deeply grateful to my divine source for the strength and guidance that have lighted my way throughout life. I also extend my heartfelt thanks to my beloveds for their constant love and support. The nurturing presence we share, along with the joyful memories we've created and will continue to create, is a never-ending source of inspiration. I love you dearly.

PREFACE

This collection is a heartfelt reflection on the journey of life, capturing the essence of its many phases through my eyes. With vivid imagery and tender emotions, it seeks to honor the timeless bonds that unite us and the exhilarating promise of the future. Each poem is a tribute to the beautiful yet bittersweet moments that define our paths, and to the relationships that illuminate and guide us along the way. This is a celebration of life's complexities, both profound and tender, and the connections that make it all worthwhile.

The Bridging Hearts

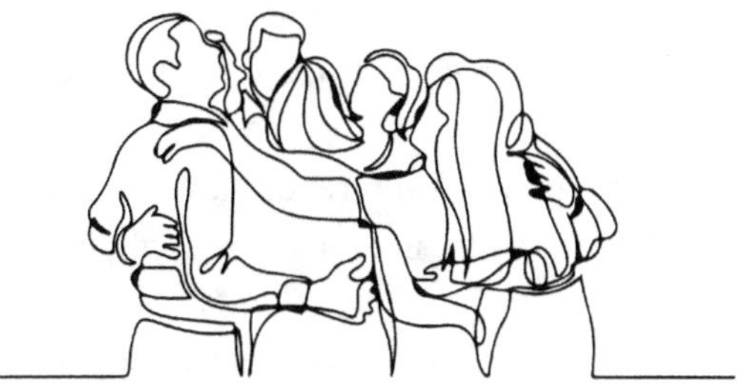

In the house where I grew, filled with laughter
and care,
Where memories of childhood float in the air,
Each corner has its stories, each wall a tale,
Of love, lessons learnt, dreams set to sail.

The mornings bright, full of sunshine and play,
Ran through the field where I used to play.
Evenings with family, warm and tight,
Love guided in the soft, gentle light.

Then you came along, my heart sang its song,
A place in your eyes where I can belong.
Our love grew strong, day and night,
A journey of joy in shared delights.

Now the day comes to declare our vows,
Mixed emotion, heart bared to the crowds.
In your arms is joy of a future so bright,
But a tear for my home in the quiet of night.

Leave the nest where I soared so high,
To build a new world with you, reaching the sky.
Happiness blooms, with a bittersweet hue,
As I cherish the past and step into the new.

Moments with family, forever they'll remain,
In my heart's depth, in dreams through joy and
pain.
Though I leave my home, I'm not on my own,
For family's love zone, in my heart, is
homegrown.

Together, hand in hand, we'll pave our way,
With yesterday's love guiding each new day.
With grace in our hearts, we'll surely rise,
A new life chapter 'neath family's loving skies.

Divine Tales of Eternal Love

In realms where sacred rivers flow,
And mountain peaks with sunlight glow,
There blooms a love, so pure, divine,
Between the gods, in holy line.

In Vishnu's eyes, the cosmos rests,
With Lakshmi by his side, so blessed,
Their love, a balance, calm and deep,
Protects the world, while mortals sleep.

On Shiva's brow, the crescent gleams,
In Parvati, his steadfast dreams,
Their union fierce, yet tender, true,
Creation's dance they both imbue.

In Krishna's flute, sweet melodies,
With Radha's grace, a gentle breeze,
Their love, a dance of joy and pain,
Eternal as the monsoon rain.

Through Ganga's flow and Yamuna's bend,
The tales of love and duty blend,
In every temple, chant, and prayer,
Their divine love is everywhere.

In sacred chants and evening lamps,
In holy texts and pilgrim camps,
The deities' love, eternal flame,
Guides every soul, through joy and pain.

For in their stories, we discern,
The ways our hearts can truly yearn,
A love that's cosmic, pure, refined,
In every prayer, their love we find.

So, under stars and temple spires,
With incense smoke and sacred fires,
We honor love that's so divine,
In every heart, the gods entwine.

Suspense and Magic in an Enchanted Forest

In twilight's glow, where magic hums,
A tale of shadows softly drums.
Whispers weave through ancient trees,
Suspense and wonder ride the breeze.

Moonlight dances on mystic ground,
Enchanted whispers all around.
A hidden path, a secret door,
To realms unseen, where legends soar.

Stars align in cryptic ways,
Casting spells in moonlit haze.
In the heart of this dark wood,
Lies a power misunderstood.

Figures cloaked in robes of night,
Cast long shadows, hearts ignite.
Mystic chants in rhythmic flow,
Guarded secrets start to grow.

Crystals gleam with ancient light,
Drawing power from the night.
In the circle, spells are cast,
Binding futures to the past.

Eyes that sparkle, deep and wise,
Hold the secrets of the skies.
Hands that weave the threads of fate,
Dance on the edge of time and space.

Whispers of an ancient lore,
Echo in the forest floor.
Mysteries deepen, shadows fall,
Magic's veil envelops all.

In this realm where wonders hide,
Suspense and magic coincide.
A world where spells and shadows blend,
In an endless tale, no end.

The Butterfly's Journey

In a meadow green and lush,
Where flowers bloom and rivers rush,
A butterfly, so light and free,
Danced amidst the willow tree.

It fluttered high, it fluttered low,
With wings aglow in sunset's glow.
A gentle breeze began to swell,
And carried with it tales to tell.

But as it soared towards the sky,
A sudden flash did catch its eye.
A portal opened, wide and bright,
And sucked it into endless night.

From meadows green to stars afar,
The butterfly became a star,
Twinkling in the cosmic sea,
A speck of light, forever free.

Echoes of Infinite Worlds

In pages bound, where whispers dwell,
I lose myself in tales they tell.
Each word a world, each line a thread,
A tapestry where dreams are spread.

The scent of paper, crisp and old,
Unlocks adventures, tales untold.
From ancient lands to future skies,
In books, a thousand lifetimes lies.

Heroes rise and villains fall,
Magic dances through it all.
In shadows deep and starlit streams,
I float away on woven dreams.

Hours slip by, unnoticed, swift,
As stories gift me time adrift.
In ink and paper, I am free,
To wander through eternity.

Symphony of Drizzle

Gentle whispers from the sky,
Soft as a lover's sigh,
In the quiet morn they lie,
A tender drizzle drifting by.

Kissing leaves with dewy grace,
A veil upon the world's face,
In each drop, a tender trace,
Of nature's gentle, sweet embrace.

Pattering on the windowpane,
A soothing song, a soft refrain,
In the hush of falling rain,
A world reborn, freed from pain.

Under gray and silver shroud,
Dreams take flight, hearts unbowed,
In the drizzle's misty crowd,
A symphony, both soft and proud.

Pressed Serenity

Steam rises in a gentle plume,
A hiss, a whisper in the room,
Wrinkles fade, their fate foredoomed,
Beneath the iron's heated bloom.

Fabric smooths beneath my hand,
Cotton, silk, at my command,
Each crease obeys the firm demand,
Of iron's touch, precise and grand.

Lines are drawn and gently pressed,
Shirts and skirts in order dressed,
In this quiet, simple quest,
A semblance of calm manifests.

In the rhythm, find the peace,
As folds and furrows find release,
Ironing clothes, a sweet caprice,
In small tasks, a soul finds ease.

Tokens of Forever

In a parchment of cream and gold,
A tale of love begins, unfolds,
A whisper of a story told,
In wedding cards, dreams are enrolled.

Ink flows in cursive, tender lines,
With words that sparkle, hearts that shine,
Invitations sent, love intertwines,
A celebration, so divine.

Ribbons tied with thoughtful care,
Delicate details everywhere,
An emblem of the joy we share,
In wedding cards, hope's answered prayer.

Each envelope, a promise made,
Of laughter, vows that won't degrade,
A journey that will never fade,
In wedding cards, love's serenade.

Sharky: the Tooth Brushing Shark

In the deep blue sea where the waves do roll,
Lived a shark named Sharky with a gleaming
goal.
Not to hunt or to frighten or to swim with might,
But to keep his teeth sparkling, oh so bright.

Every morning with the rising sun,
Sharky grabbed his brush, the routine had begun.
With a splash and a swish, he'd scrub each tooth,
From his mighty molars to his pearly youth.

The fish would giggle, the crabs would cheer,
"Look at Sharky, his teeth so clear!"
He'd hum a tune, as he'd brush along,
A bubbly rhythm, a toothy song.

No plaque, no grime, no fishy breath,
Sharky's smile was the best in the ocean's
breadth.
He'd teach the young ones, with a glint in his
eye,
"Brush twice a day, and you'll reach the sky!"

So if you swim by, and see a glistening gleam,
It's Sharky the Shark, living his dream.
With a toothbrush in fin, and a grin so wide,
Sharky's the cleanest shark in the tide.

A Door to Yesterday

Once upon a time, when days were bright,
And the sun would smile with all its might,
You'd play in fields, so green and wide,
With friends and laughter, side by side.

Remember the swings, so high they flew,
And the secret places only you knew?
The ice cream truck with its jolly tune,
And chasing fireflies under the moon.

These memories, like treasures, stay,
In a special place where time can't sway.
They're like old toys, a bit worn out,
But filled with joy, without a doubt.

Nostalgia's like a magic door,
To days and moments we adore.
It's a way to visit the past so dear,
And keep those happy times near.

So hold those memories in your heart,
They're pieces of you, a special part.
And when you feel them start to glow,
That's nostalgia, just saying hello.

Wings on Hold

In the airport, waiting still,
Time seems paused, against our will.
The board reads "Delayed," the hours slow,
To Melbourne, we're late, nowhere to go.

Travelers sigh, in quiet dismay,
As minutes turn to hours in disarray.
But dreams of Melbourne keep us bright,
Through the long and endless night.

Soon we'll soar, leave delays behind,
And touch the skies with peace of mind.
For every journey has its way,
Even those that go astray.

Mystery of Stars

In the quiet of the night so deep,
Stars awaken from their cosmic sleep.
They twinkle secrets in the sky,
Mysteries hidden way up high.

Ancient stories, whispers old,
Tales of wonder they silently hold.
Guiding travelers through the dark,
Each one a bright, celestial spark.

What do they see from their lofty height?
Guardians of the endless night.
Stars keep their secrets, near and far,
The timeless mystery of every star.

The Universal Language of Laughter

Laughter is a joyful sound,
That knows no age, it's always found.
In a child's giggle, pure and sweet,
Or friends who laugh when they meet.

A chuckle shared by those who're young,
Or hearty laughs from old, well-spun.
Middle-aged find humor's grace,
A smile can light up any face.

It breaks the ice, it heals the heart,
From life's worries, it sets apart.
A joke, a pun, or silly play,
Can brighten up the darkest day.

No matter where, no matter who,
Laughter is a bond so true.
So let it echo, near and far,
The universal joy we are.

The Dance of the Skies

In the sky, we soar so high,
Among the clouds, where dreams can fly.
Then turbulence, a sudden shake,
A dance of nature, make no mistake.

Winds will twist and currents turn,
Lessons in the air to learn.
The plane will dip, then rise anew,
Through unseen waves of sky so blue.

It's like a waltz, a rhythmic beat,
A moment where calm and chaos meet.
But in the beauty of the ride,
We find our trust, we set aside.

For every jolt, a thrill is born,
A reminder in the early morn,
That even in the roughest air,
There's beauty, wonder, everywhere.

So, as we glide through skies untamed,
With hearts that feel both fear and famed,
We see the beauty in the sway,
Of nature's power, at play each day.

Whispers Through Time

Through the veil of years we stride,
In a time machine, we glide.
Back to days of olden lore,
Or future realms, we explore.

The past unfolds, a silent scroll,
Moments lost, now make us whole.
We meet the legends, face to face,
In distant lands, in a different place.

To the future, bright and grand,
Where dreams are built on shifting sand.
We see the world that's yet to be,
A tapestry of mystery.

Every tick and every tock,
Unlocks the door with a gentle knock.
We travel through the streams of time,
In a dance, both grand and sublime.

Yet in our hearts, we always find,
The present moment, intertwined.
For time's a river, ever-flowing,
A journey endless, never knowing.

So as we wander, far and near,
Through days of joy and nights of fear,
We cherish time, both near and far,
Our guiding light, our shining star.

Chatter and Calm

I'm a chatterbox, full of glee,
Words flow freely, wild and free.
Stories, laughter, endless streams,
A lively world of vivid dreams.

My husband, quiet, gentle, kind,
With a thoughtful, loving mind.
Polite and calm, he speaks so soft,
A soothing presence, tender, aloft.

He loves my chatter, bright and loud,
The way I animate a crowd.
He listens with a patient smile,
Enjoying every word and style.

And I adore his quiet grace,
The peaceful aura in his space.
His introverted, sweet embrace,
A love so gentle, sets the pace.

Together, we are perfectly matched,
A bond so strong, securely latched.
In his calm, I find my rest,
In my chatter, he feels blessed.

Two hearts in harmony, we blend,
A lovely balance, a perfect friend.
Our love a dance, both loud and still,
Chatter and calm, forever will.

Echoes of Debate

Since sixteen years, my voice found flight,
In halls of discourse, sharp and bright.
Where ideas clash and minds ignite,
Debates, my passion, my guiding light.

In circles grand, with fervent flair,
Arguments woven with utmost care.
Logic sharp, like a sculptor's knife,
Carving truths from the stone of life.

Each topic, a mountain to ascend,
With every point, a chance to mend.
Opinions formed, convictions strong,
In the dance of words, I belong.

I stand my ground, with courage bold,
In heated moments, stories told.
Facts and figures, woven tight,
In the arena, I find my light.

For debate is not just clash and fight,
It's the pursuit of what is right.
A quest for truth, a noble game,
Where every voice holds a flame.

Immersed in this, my spirit flies,
Through every argument and rise.
Debates, my stage, my heartfelt art,
A journey that began from the start.

With every word, a chance to grow,
To see the world and better know.
For in the dialogue, hearts expand,
And through debate, I firmly stand.

The Magical Rhythm

In melodies that gently rise,
A world unfolds before our eyes.
Notes that dance upon the air,
A touch of magic everywhere.

Strings that hum and keys that sing,
In every chord, new worlds they bring.
A rhythm steady, a beat so true,
Music weaves its spell on you.

In moments soft and symphonies grand,
A universal language, hand in hand.
It lifts the spirit, soothes the mind,
A treasure for the heart to find.

From lullabies that calm the night,
To anthems bold that spark the fight,
Every tune a story shares,
Of love and dreams and worldly cares.

Close your eyes and let it flow,
Feel the magic start to grow.
In every note, a secret lies,
A gentle whisper, a sweet surprise.

For music holds the power to heal,
To paint the world with what we feel.
In every song, our souls take flight,
A boundless journey, pure delight.

So, let the music fill the space,
With its tender, warm embrace.
The magic of music, always near,
A symphony for the heart to hear.

Crowning Dreams

In childhood days, so bright and fair,
I dreamed a dream beyond compare.
To grace the stage with poise and grace,
A sparkling crown, a beaming face.

Miss World, a title grand and pure,
A vision in my heart, so sure.
With every step, I held the dream,
A shining star in my youthful gleam.

In mirror's reflection, I'd see,
A future self, confident and free.
Practicing my walk and smile,
Imagining the grandest aisle.

A dream of beauty, heart, and mind,
To inspire, uplift, and be kind.
A voice for change, a hand to lend,
To be a guide, a trusted friend.

From pageant gowns to heartfelt words,
Dreams took flight like soaring birds.
Each question answered with a thought,
A journey that my heart had sought.

Though time has passed, the dream remains,
A testament to childhood gains.
For in that dream, I found my spark,
A light that brightens up the dark.

Miss World, a dream that shaped my days,
In every challenge, through every phase.
A childhood wish, a guiding star,
That dream lives on, no matter how far.

Fruity Tuesdays

Every Tuesday, dawn's first light,
Brings a ritual, pure and bright.
A day devoted to fruits alone,
A feast of nature, simply grown.

Apples crisp and berries sweet,
A wholesome, vibrant, weekly treat.
Bananas, mangoes, citrus bliss,
Each bite, a moment of pure kiss.

In every slice, a burst of life,
Free from worry, free from strife.
Nature's bounty, fresh and pure,
A mindful practice to endure.

Grapes that burst with juicy cheer,
Pineapple, tangy, brings me near.
To nature's essence, raw and real,
A connection deep, a heartfelt meal.

With every fruit, my body sings,
Renewal felt, like gentle springs.
A pause from life's incessant beat,
To savor nature's simple treat.

This weekly fast, a cherished part,
Of nurturing my mind and heart.
A day of fruits, so bright and true,
A gift each Tuesday, fresh and new.

For in this practice, strength I find,
A clarity that cleanses the mind.
Tuesday's fruit fast, my sacred time,
A weekly ritual, pure and sublime.

Sacred Visit To Puttaparthi

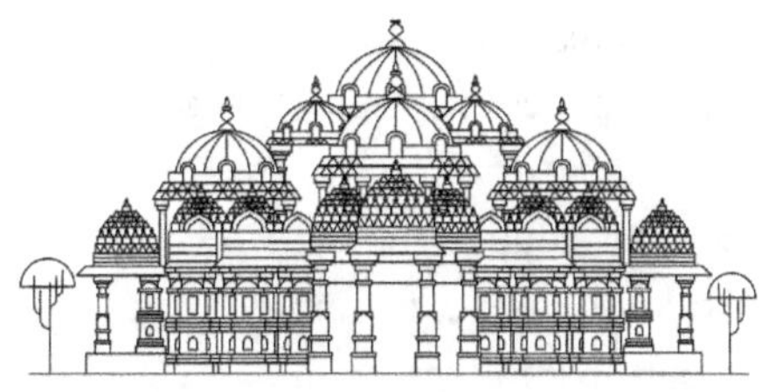

To Puttaparthi, a sacred land,
Where peace and grace together stand.
Sathya Sai Baba's ashram bright,
A beacon of divine light.

We journeyed there with hearts so wide,
To feel the love that can't be denied.
In every corner, whispers sweet,
Of devotion pure, our spirits greet.

The air is filled with prayers and song,
A place where souls feel they belong.
In gardens lush and temples grand,
We feel the touch of a divine hand.

Pilgrims gather, near and far,
Guided by that shining star.
In silence deep, in chants so clear,
Sathya Sai Baba's presence near.

The ashram glows with serene light,
A refuge from the worldly fight.
Here, in this hallowed, tranquil space,
We find our peace, our inner grace.

His teachings echo in the air,
A call to love, to live, to care.
In Puttaparthi's holy ground,
A deeper truth, our hearts have found.

Leaving with our spirits high,
Under the vast and gentle sky.
Puttaparthi stays within our heart,
A place where earthly woes depart.

A New Dawn in a Foreign Land

Bags are packed, the world awaits,
A journey calls, a twist of fates.
Home fades behind, dreams ahead,
A new chapter begins, where paths are tread.

The plane ascends, the heart does too,
Eyes wide open, skies turn blue.
Familiar comforts left behind,
A foreign land, a new design.

Unknown streets, yet they seem alive,
A language strange, yet words survive.
Smiles and nods bridge the gap,
A handshake firm, a friendly tap.

Roots are planted where feet now stand,
New soil, new dreams, a foreign strand.
A place once strange begins to grow,
In its embrace, a heart aglow.

The winds may whisper of days gone by,
Of laughter shared, a tear to dry.
Yet forward steps the soul must take,
A world to build, a life to make.

For in this land of endless skies,
A future blooms, a phoenix rise.
Relocation is not an end,
It's where the soul learns to transcend.

The Whispering Forest

Beneath the canopy's emerald glow,
A symphony of rustling, soft and low.
The trees lean close, their secrets shared,
In whispered tones, with hearts unbarred.

Each root a story, each leaf a dream,
Flowing with life in a timeless stream.
The forest hums with ancient lore,
A living world, forevermore.

The Flickering Flame

A single candle in the night,
A fragile dance of golden light.
Its glow defies the darkest hue,
A beacon bright, a hope renewed.

The flame may falter, the winds may roar,
But steadfast it burns, its spirit more.
For even in its fleeting glow,
A warmth persists, a love will grow.

The Ocean's Song

The ocean sings in rhythmic waves,
A tune that heals, a heart enslaves.
Its voice is vast, both wild and free,
A ceaseless hymn of mystery.

The shore embraces each ebb, each flow,
Its sands adorned with tales of woe.
Yet in its depths, life's treasures hide,
A realm untamed, the sea's great pride.

The Timekeeper's Clock

Tick, tock, the hours chime,
A constant beat through space and time.
Its hands move slow, yet never cease,
A steady march of fleeting peace.

Each tick a moment, each tock a chance,
To weave life's tale, a fleeting dance.
The clock reminds with every tone,
That time is ours, yet not our own.

Whispers of the Moon

Beneath the moon's soft silver hue,
Two hearts unite, a love so true.
The stars above, a sparkling choir,
Ignite the night with gentle fire.

The breeze that carries whispered vows,
Dances softly through the boughs.
The world fades away, it's only them,
Bound by love, their night a gem.

The Bloom of Us

Like petals kissed by morning dew,
Our love grows fresh, forever new.
In fields of gold, we laugh, we play,
A bond that blossoms every day.

Each moment shared, a fragrant bloom,
Banishing shadows, brightening gloom.
Together we thrive, like nature's art,
A garden planted heart to heart.

Eternal Rivers

Love flows gently, a river wide,
With every twist, our souls collide.
Its waters sing a tender song,
Guiding us both where we belong.

Through rocky paths, its current glides,
A bond unbroken, the stream abides.
Forever it flows, through time, through space,
An endless journey, a sweet embrace.

A Symphony of Seasons

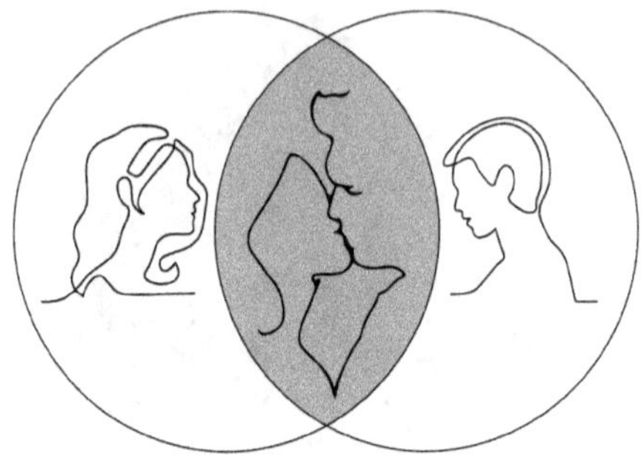

Through spring's soft blush, our love takes
flight,
In summer's glow, it burns so bright.
When autumn falls, with golden hue,
We dance through leaves, both me and you.

Winter comes with frosty air,
Yet in your arms, I'm unaware.
Each season brings its own delight,
With you, my world is pure and right.

In Nature's Arms

We walked through woods, hand in hand,
Our footprints kissed the soft, warm sand.
The waves serenade, the trees hum low,
Nature's love, a gentle flow.

Your smile, the sun, that lights my day,
Your voice, the wind, that guides my way.
In every leaf, in every stream,
I find your love, a perfect dream.

The Shattered Kite

A kite once flew in skies so high,
A child below with dreams to try.
But winds grew fierce, the string did snap,
The sky turned gray, the world fell flat.

Tiny hands reached, but dreams were torn,
A heart once pure began to mourn.
Yet through the tears, a will took flight,
To mend the string, to brave the night.

The Empty Desk

A classroom buzzed with laughter loud,
But one child sat beneath the crowd.
A desk with books, but no one near,
Loneliness etched, a silent fear.

From teasing words to looks askew,
A fragile soul each day withdrew.
Yet in the quiet, strength was born,
To rise above, to face the scorn.

The Weight of a Door

Behind closed doors, the echoes rang,
Of broken voices, anger's pang.
A child who longed for warmth, for peace,
Found solace fleeting, a brief release.

The weight of silence, heavy and true,
Shaped a heart both brave and blue.
And though the scars of youth remain,
The spirit learned to bear the pain.

Adulthood came, a balancing act,
A tightrope stretched, a life compact.
With bills to pay and dreams to keep,
A soul once wild grew worn, grew steep.

The child within still dared to run,
But burdens blocked the fleeting sun.
Yet step by step, the rope held strong,
For hardship carves where we belong.

The River Within

A river ran through years of strife,
From childhood woes to adult life.
Its currents swirled with pain and fear,
Yet whispered hope through every tear.

The bends were sharp, the waters cold,
But deeper truths began to unfold.
For even rivers carved by pain,
Lead to oceans where dreams sustain.

The Tightrope Walk

Adulthood arrived, a constant strain,
A tightrope walk through joy and pain.
With bills to pay and dreams to chase,
The wild soul slowed in life's embrace.

The child inside still longed to play,
But heavy loads clouded the day.
Yet, inch by inch, the rope stayed true,
For struggles shape the path we pursue.

Bound by Fire

We are the flame, both light and heat,
A dance of love, a clash we meet.
Passion burns bright, yet sparks ignite,
A bond of beauty, a constant fight.

The Push and Pull

We draw together, then drift apart,
A tug of war inside the heart.
In love, we thrive, in hate, we break,
Yet always find the paths we take.

The Storm Inside Us

Your words, like rain, they pierce and heal,
A tempest wild, a love so real.
Through lightning strikes and thunder's roar,
We crave each other, wanting more.

Glass and Stone

You shatter me, I cut you deep,
Our wounds are raw, our scars we keep.
Yet in the cracks, light filters through,
Revealing love still strong, still true.

The Echo of Us

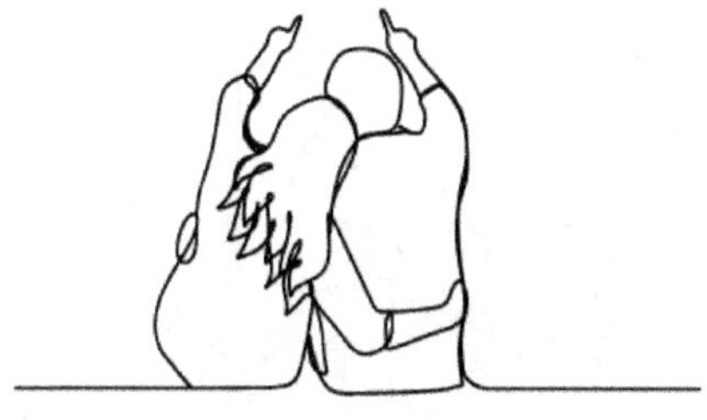

In love, we whisper, in hate, we scream,
Caught between a nightmare and a dream.
Yet even when the echoes fade,
Our souls are bound, the choice we made.

The Pendulum

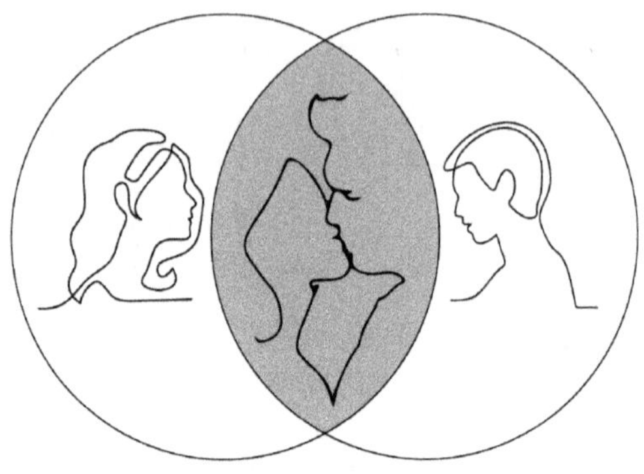

We swing between the joy and pain,
A cycle endless, love's refrain.
Hate pulls us down, yet love will rise,
A constant battle beneath the skies.

Tangled Threads

Our hearts are threads, both frayed and tight,
Entwined in day, unspooled by night.
Each knot we tie, each string we tear,
Leaves marks of love and hate we share.

The Poison and the Cure

You are the venom, yet the balm,
My raging storm, my soothing calm.
The pain you bring, the joy you give,
In this paradox, we choose to live.

Shadows of Us

In every smile, a hidden tear,
In every embrace, a lingering fear.
Love and hate, like shadows play,
Together they guide our way.

Through the Flames

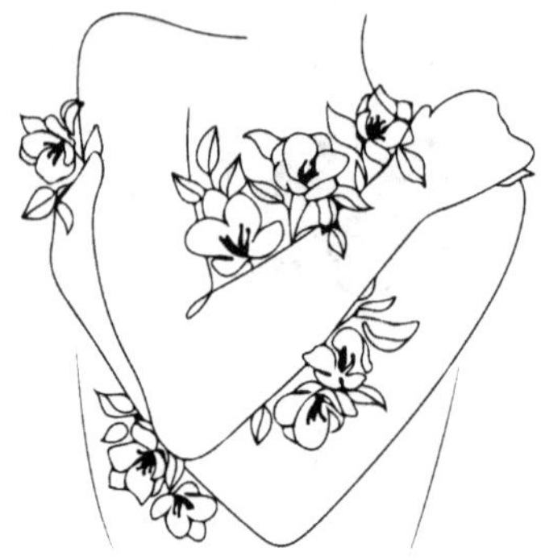

Our love's a fire, fierce and bright,
Yet hate consumes in the darkest night.
Through ashes, we rebuild once more,
Forever seeking the love we swore.

Love

The Language of Hearts
Words unspoken, yet understood,
A bond so pure, a love so good.
In your arms, the world makes sense,
A timeless tale, love's recompense.

Infinite Us

Through time and space, our souls align,
A love eternal, a spark divine.
No force can break, no tide can sway,
Together we're infinite, come what may.

Innocent Days

Beneath the tree where shadows played,
We laughed and dreamed, in sunlight stayed.
A love so pure, without a care,
In childhood's glow, we found it there.

Paper Hearts

Notes passed in class, a secret smile,
A love that bloomed in the simplest style.
Though years have passed, those days remain,
A tender ache, a sweet refrain.

The Ring of Promise

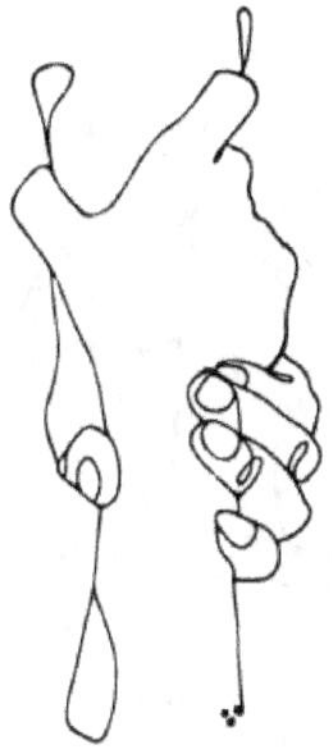

A circle of gold, a vow to keep,
A bond so strong, a love so deep.
With this ring, a journey starts,
Two souls entwined, two beating hearts.

Forever Begins

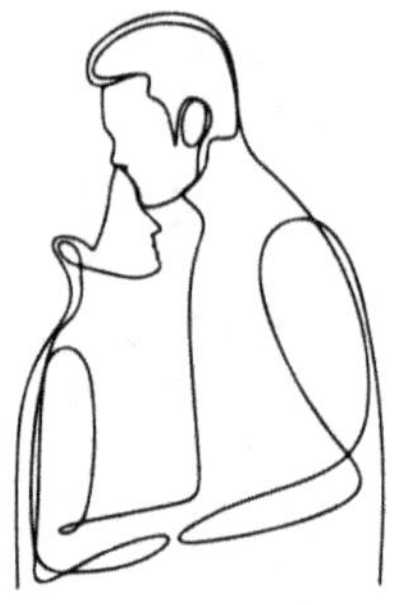

On this day, a promise made,
In love's embrace, we'll never fade.
Through trials and joys, we'll stand as one,
Our journey starts; forever's begun.

The Wedding Vows

Under the arch, with skies so wide,
Two hearts unite, two souls abide.
Through tears and joy, we boldly say,
"I choose you, forever and a day."

A Union Divine

Families gather, hands are clasped,
A love eternal, tightly grasped.
With every step, our bond takes flight,
A sacred vow in love's pure light.

A New Home Beckons

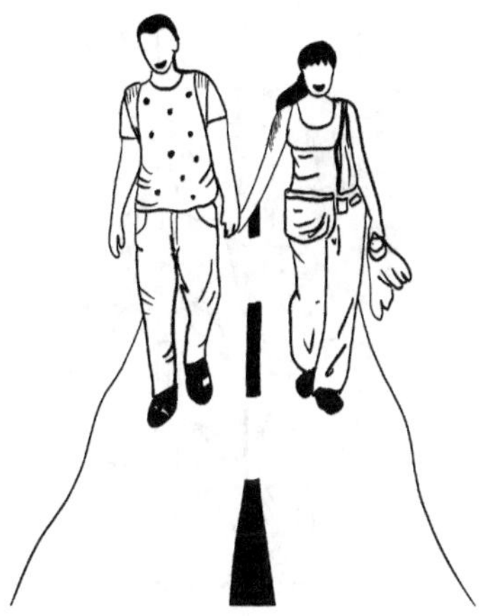

Shalom calls from distant shores,
A land of history, a place of yours.
Through ancient stones, your roots are found,
A sacred space, a hallowed ground.

Embracing the Culture

Through Hebrew words and sacred song,
You find a place where you belong.
Traditions guide, your spirit free,
A life renewed in this journey.

Unfamiliar Streets

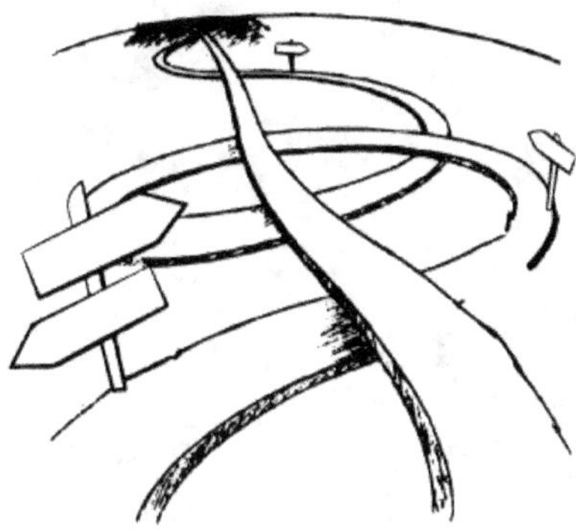

New paths to walk, new hands to greet,
The world feels strange, yet bittersweet.
Through every turn, you find your way,
Adjustments bloom with each new day.

The Comfort of Change

The days are foreign, yet they bring,
The joy of growth, the strength to cling.
Each challenge faced, a story made,
A brighter self, in changes laid.

Thankful Heart

For every sunrise, every chance,
For life's great song, its endless dance.
I thank the stars, the earth, the sea,
For love, for you, for being me.

Grateful Steps

Each step I take, a blessing known,
Each seed of love, so deeply sown.
I walk through life with joy to spare,
Grateful for all, beyond compare.

Childhood to Now

From childhood games to wedding vows,
Life has brought us here and now.
Through every stage, our love has grown,
A life together, seeds we've sown.

A Life Transformed

New lands, new love, a story new,
Through all of this, I've grown with you.
Adjustments made with open hearts,
Grateful for all that life imparts.

Sacred Love

In sacred halls, our love took flight,
Through faith and trust, we found the light.
The culture rich, the ties that bind,
A love so strong, a peace we find.

From Then to Now

From childish dreams to wedding days,
Through love and growth, we found our ways.
Each moment built on those before,
A journey rich, with love and more.

The Journey Together

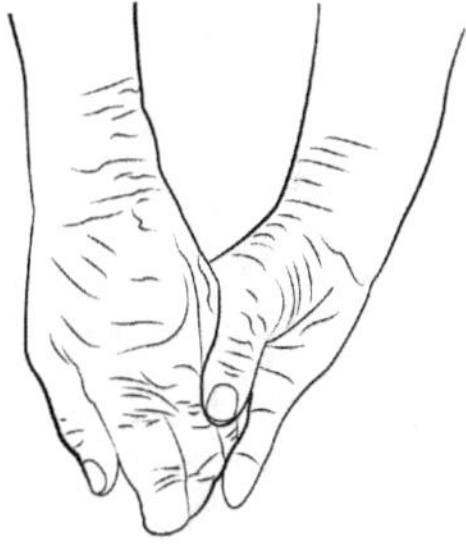

Through moves, through vows, through love's
embrace,
You are my home, my sacred space.
Each trial faced with hands held tight,
Together, we'll weather any night.

The Us We Built

In every change, in every storm,
Our love has kept us safe and warm.
Grateful for you, for all we share,
A life of love, beyond compare.

The Tapestry of Us

Threads of love, of faith, of dreams,
A woven life, a golden seam.
Through every change, our story grows,
Grateful for all, as life bestows.

Rooted in Love

Like trees that grow through wind and rain,
Our love endures through joy and pain.
Rooted deep, our bond will stay,
Through every night, through every day.

A Guiding Star

Through darkened skies, your light shines true,
A beacon bright, a love so new.
Grateful am I for all you are,
My constant, my guide, my shining star.

Looking Ahead

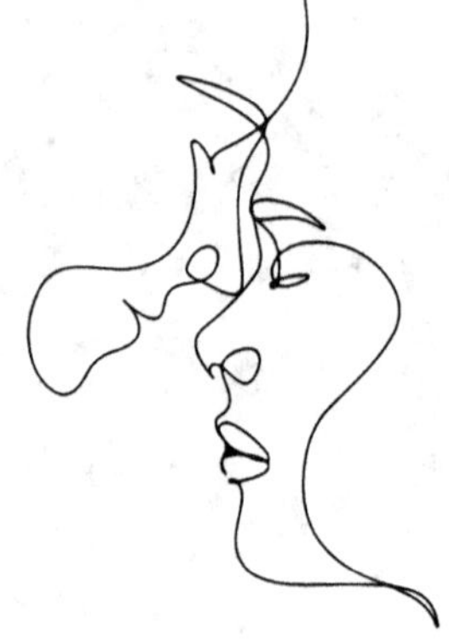

With each new day, our story unfolds,
A love so vast, too great to hold.
Through every turn, through every bend,
Grateful for you, my love, my friend.

Forever Grateful

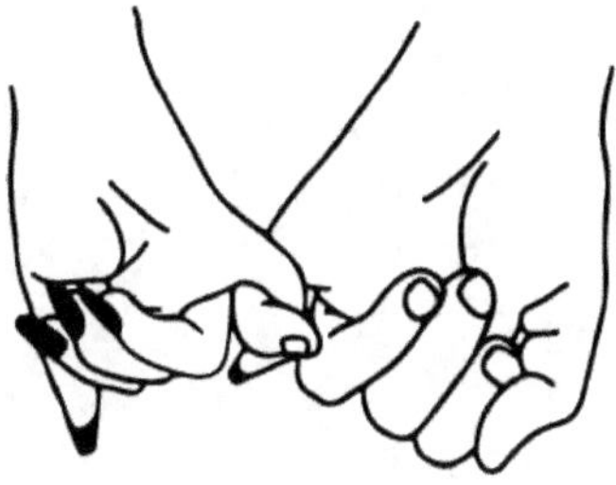

For love, for life, for every kiss,
For every moment filled with bliss.
I thank the heavens, the stars above,
For giving me you, my endless love.

www.ingramcontent.com/pod-product-compliance
Lightning Source LLC
La Vergne TN
LVHW011038200726
843509LV00011B/1311